CAN'T I JUST WANT SOMETHING

More?

A Career Change Guide for People Who Aren't Starting from Scratch

Jennifer Larsen

Originality Statement

This book is an original work written by the author and reflects their unique ideas, voice, and instructional approach. While it may reference common educational and career-planning concepts, all content, including structure, language, exercises, and framework, is the author's own creation. Any similarities to other published works are purely coincidental.

Printed in the United States of America

ISBN: 978-1-968756-75-8

First Edition

Cover design by Rachel Bostwick

Interior design and layout by Rachel Bostwick

For information or bulk orders, visit cantijust.com

Contents

Introduction:

What If It's Not Too Late to Want Something More?

Maybe you're not "miserable."

Maybe your job looks fine on paper.

Maybe you've even got a few people wondering why you'd ever think of leaving it.

But still – something's off.

You're burned out, bored, or just plain tired. You've outgrown the box you're in, and no amount of stretching seems to make it fit again.

If you've ever stared at your ceiling wondering if this is all there is... you're not alone. And you're not crazy.

This book is for *you*.

💡 What You're Feeling Isn't Failure

You don't have to hit rock bottom to want something better.

You don't need a dramatic event to justify change.

And you don't need anyone's permission – least of all the version of yourself who made a career decision 15 years ago when life looked very different.

Shifting gears in midlife isn't reckless.

It's *smart*. It means you've grown enough to ask the right questions.

This Isn't a Reinvention Story

We're not here to pressure you into becoming a whole new person.

This isn't one of those "Quit everything! Follow your passion!" books.

Instead, we'll build a quiet, confident bridge — from where you are now, to what's next.

Using what you already know. What you already value.

And what you *might* still be dreaming about when nobody's watching.

✓ What You'll Find Here

This book walks you through the midlife shift **emotionally first**, then practically.

Because if you've ever tried to leap straight into "solutions" while your brain was still spinning, you already know: it doesn't work.

Here's how we'll move:

1. **Emotional first** – Grief, fear, identity, self-doubt

2. **Reframe** – What you want now vs what you used to want

3. **Tools** – Skills inventory, fit tests, flexibility models

4. **Action** – Résumé pivots, career redesign, planning forward

You don't need to go fast.

You just need to go *honestly*.

✳ Let's Walk This Together

You're not starting from scratch.

You're starting from experience.

And the person you've become?

They deserve a career that fits the life you're building now — not the life you left behind.

📖 Chapter One: Is This It?

Maybe it's been creeping up on you for years.

Maybe it hit you in the middle of folding laundry.

A little voice that whispers:

"Is this really what I'm doing with the rest of my life?"

At first, you try to brush it off.

You're lucky, right? You have a job. You're good at it. Maybe it even pays well.

But the whisper doesn't go away.

It starts showing up in the middle of staff meetings. In the car. On Sunday nights.

You find yourself mentally checking out... but you don't know what you're checking *into*.

💡 This Isn't a Crisis – It's a Signal

That nagging feeling you keep trying to ignore?

It's not rebellion. It's not immaturity. It's not failure.

It's a signal.

It means **you've outgrown something**.

And it's okay to outgrow things. Even if they're decent. Even if they made sense once.

Especially if you've changed – and chances are, *you have.*

You've learned what you can tolerate, what you hate, what lights you up, and what drains you in 30 seconds flat.

You've also spent years molding yourself to fit into systems that weren't built for who you are now.

Of course something feels off.

✓ Why This Matters

You can't make a change you don't name.

And if you keep chalking your discomfort up to stress, or over-work, or "just needing a vacation,"

you'll miss the actual invitation:

It's time to figure out what's next.

That doesn't mean quitting your job tomorrow.

It means giving yourself permission to listen to the part of you that's tired of pretending you're fine.

Because *fine* isn't the same as fulfilled.

And surviving isn't the same as living.

❓ Ask Yourself:

- What part of my current work feels the most like a mask?
- When do I feel most like myself?
- If no one else's opinion mattered, what would I admit I want?

You don't have to know the answers yet.

You just have to stop acting like the questions aren't there.

📌 Try This: Track the "Ick"

Over the next week, jot down the moments at work when you feel:

- Dread

- Discomfort

- Boredom

- Anger

- That heavy pit-in-the-stomach vibe

You don't have to do anything with the list yet.

Just name it. Patterns will emerge – and they'll matter later.

▼ **Bottom Line:**

You're not broken. You're just done pretending that "this is fine" means "this is right."

Something inside you is starting to shift.

You don't need to fix it.

You just need to **follow it**.

Chapter Two:

When You Can't Tell If It's Grief or Burnout

You've probably asked yourself more than once:

"Am I just tired, or is something actually wrong?"

It's a fair question.

Because some days you feel fried.

Other days, you feel lost.

And some days, you feel nothing at all – just blank.

What you're experiencing might look like burnout on the surface.

But underneath, it's often **grief**.

Grief for:

- The version of you who thought this path would feel different
- The time you can't get back
- The identity you built around being "good" at something that doesn't fit anymore
- The people you outgrew – or who outgrew you

🕯 This Isn't Melodrama. It's Reality.

When a job has been part of your identity for years – maybe decades –

it's not just a task list you're walking away from.

It's a whole *chapter of yourself.*

Letting go of that chapter can feel like death, even if it's the right thing to do.

You may not be mourning a person.

But you're mourning stability. Predictability. A sense of self.

And the world doesn't always give you permission to do that.

So instead of grieving, you push through. You tell yourself it's burnout. That you'll bounce back.

But deep down? You already know you're not going back to how it was.

⚠ How Burnout and Grief Can Look the Same

Sometimes it's both.

And sometimes, one hides behind the other.

⚙ The Trickiest Part? You Don't Know What to Mourn.

This isn't like losing a person.

It's fuzzier. Harder to name.

You're not even sure what, exactly, you're grieving.

But you feel it in your bones:

- That ache when you remember how excited you used to be

- That envy when someone else lights up about *their* work

- That guilt when your partner asks what's wrong and you don't have an answer

You don't need to name it perfectly to acknowledge it.

You just need to **let it matter.**

Try This: Name the Losses

Write down what you think you're grieving. Even if it sounds silly.

Even if you're not sure it "counts."

Try these prompts:

- "I thought I'd still be _____ by now."

- "I miss how it used to feel when _____."

- "It hurts that I no longer _____."

- "I'm embarrassed that _____."

Don't try to solve it.

Just put it down where you can see it.

This is the emotional housekeeping that makes room for whatever's next.

▼ Bottom Line:

You might not be burned out – you might just be sad.
And sadness doesn't mean you're wrong for wanting more.

Give yourself a moment to honor what's ending.

You don't have to rush toward what's next.
But you *do* have to stop pretending you're fine.

⊡ *Chapter Three:*

When You're Not Starting Over (But It Feels Like It)

Let's get something straight up front:

You are not starting from scratch.

Even if you change your job, your field, your routine, your whole damn life...

you are not the same person you were at 20.

And thank god.

But that doesn't mean it *feels* easy.

When you're looking at a blank slate – especially after decades in a career – it can feel like you're back at the bottom. Like you've lost ground. Like you somehow failed.

You haven't.

What you're really doing is **leveraging everything you've learned so far** – not tossing it.

✂ You've Been Building This All Along

Here's what nobody tells you:

You've been gathering the pieces for this shift *for years.*

Every awkward meeting, every bad boss, every weird project that taught you something you didn't expect – it's all in the pile.

That pile might not look organized yet. But it holds:

- Experience you don't even realize you have

- Patterns you've already noticed (what drains you, what energizes you)

- People who respect you more than you think

- Resilience you built without asking for it

You are not at square one.

You're just standing in a new part of the board.

Your Toolkit's Already Packed

When people say "start over," they picture themselves naked on the battlefield.

But you? You've got gear.

You know how to:

- Read the room
- Write an email that actually gets answered
- Lead a conversation
- Take rejection and keep going
- Deliver under pressure
- Deal with people (even the worst ones)

Even if your next step feels wildly different on paper, you're not going in unarmed.

🧠 The Mental Loop: "But I Don't Want to Waste My Past"

This one shows up a lot:

"I've put so much time into this. If I leave, was it all for nothing?"

No. It wasn't.

You weren't wasting time. You were gaining **clarity**.

That job you can't stand?

It taught you what to never tolerate again.

That career path that lost its spark?

It helped you build the confidence to try something new.

This is *not* the beginning.

It's a new season – and you're entering it better equipped than ever.

Try This: Inventory of Usefulness

Think back over your last few jobs, even the bad ones.

Ask yourself:

- What skills did I develop (hard *and* soft)?
- What insights did I gain about myself?
- What people did I meet who I'd still want in my corner?
- What do I never want to do again?

Write it down.

This is your foundation. You're not starting over. You're **starting from experience.**

▦ Bonus Exercise: Sort Your Strengths

Now that you've listed what you've learned, let's sort that list using a method called MoSCoW – just not the way project managers do it.

Label each item using these categories:

- **Must** – These are strengths you want to *definitely* use in your next chapter. They light you up or give you serious leverage.

- **Should** – These are things you're good at, but you'd like to use a little less – or on your terms.

- **Could** – These are bonus skills. Nice to have, but not a priority.

- **Won't** – These are the things you're done with. No more. Period.

This sorting helps you **spot patterns, eliminate baggage**, and start thinking like someone who's already got a head start – which you do.

▼ Bottom Line:

You're not failing. You're evolving.

Everything you've done has brought you here.
And even if this next step looks unfamiliar, you're not lost.

You're just **ready** – even if you don't feel like it yet.

Chapter Four:

When You Don't Know What You Want Yet

It's one of the worst feelings –

that moment when someone asks, *"Well, what do you want to do instead?"*

...and your brain goes completely blank.

You don't know.

You used to know.

You used to have plans. Dreams. Maybe even backup dreams.

Now?

You're just tired.

You've outgrown what you were doing –

but you haven't grown into something else yet.

This Is What the Middle Feels Like

You're not at the beginning of your life.

You're not at the end of your career.

You're somewhere in between – where the old identity doesn't fit,

but the new one hasn't shown up yet.

This isn't failure.

This is **transition**.

And transitions are messy.

They're murky and uncomfortable. They make you question everything.

They don't move in a straight line.

And they sure as hell don't move on your timeline.

When You've Been Focused on Survival, Desire Gets Quiet

Let's be honest: a lot of people don't know what they want because they've spent years focused on:

- Paying bills
- Raising kids
- Getting through
- Avoiding risk
- Keeping things "good enough"

That's not laziness.

That's life.

But after enough time, you stop asking yourself what you want.

You get good at **managing**, but not dreaming.

So when you *finally* get the space to ask that question again – "What do I want?" – you come up empty.

That's not because there's nothing in you.

It's because the signal is buried under years of noise.

💼 You Don't Need a Dream Job. You Need a Clue.

Let's take the pressure off.

You're not looking for your "one true calling" here.

You're just looking for the **next breadcrumb**. A hint. A spark. Something that makes you lean forward just a little.

What makes you curious?

What feels satisfying when you finish it?

What feels like play instead of work?

Start there. Not with the résumé. With the feeling.

📝 Try This:
The "I Don't Know, But – " List

Grab a notebook or open a doc. Fill in the blanks:

- I don't know what I want, but I know I'm tired of
  _____.

- I don't know what I'm aiming for, but I feel pulled toward _____.

- I don't know what the job is, but I want to feel _____
  at the end of the day.

- I don't know what success looks like anymore, but it
  probably doesn't include _____.

This is how you **start listening** to yourself again.

You don't need a full map.

You just need a direction.

▼ **Bottom Line:**

You're not broken because you don't have a dream right now.
You're healing.

And once the noise clears, you'll start to hear your own voice
again.

That voice is still in there.
It's just waiting for you to ask what *you* want – without judgment.

Chapter Five:

When You're Scared to Choose Wrong

"What if I make the leap...and regret it?"

"What if I go down the wrong path and waste even more time?"

"What if I mess this up worse than before?"

You're not lazy.

You're not flaky.

You're **scared of wasting your life.**

That fear shows up as hesitation, perfectionism, over-researching, stalling.

It's your brain's way of trying to protect you.

But if you're not careful, "figuring it out" can turn into a **permanent pause**.

⚉ Fear of the Wrong Choice Keeps You Stuck in No Choice

There's this myth that one perfect path is out there.

You just have to find it. And if you don't, you'll regret everything.

Here's what's more likely true:

- There are *several* good paths for you

- Most things aren't permanent

- You can course-correct at any age

- The wrong thing teaches you the right thing faster than sitting still ever will

But none of that matters if fear is still running the show.

The Real Question Isn't "Is This Right?" It's "Can I Learn From This?"

A better goal than "get it right" is:

"Choose something I can grow from."

Ask yourself:

- Does this option excite me, even if it's scary?

- Would I be proud to try, even if it doesn't last forever?

- Will this help me figure out what fits *better* – even if it's not perfect?

That's not a mistake. That's **movement**.

🏃 Action Builds Clarity (Not the Other Way Around)

People think clarity comes first, then action.

But often it's the **other way around**.

- You try something new
- You discover what feels good and what doesn't
- You adjust
- You learn more about yourself
- You pivot again
- Repeat

That's not flailing. That's how real adult reinvention works.

Try This: Fear vs Curiosity

Draw two columns.

Label the first one **"Fear Says..."** and the second one **"Curiosity Says..."**

Now complete these based on your current situation:

The goal isn't to eliminate fear.

It's to turn up the volume on curiosity – so it can *speak louder.*

▼ Bottom Line:

You don't need to be fearless to move forward.

You just need to be brave *enough* to try.

Choosing something isn't the trap.

Staying frozen is.

And most people regret what they *didn't* try — not what they did.

Chapter Six

When You're Still Not Sure You're Allowed to Want More

You've built a life.

You've checked the boxes.

You've done the "right" things — maybe even the hard things.

And now, here you are...

Still wanting something else.

Not because you're ungrateful.

Not because you're impulsive.

But because something inside you *knows* there's still more out there.

And it feels like a betrayal to say it out loud.

😔 Guilt Keeps You Quiet

You start asking yourself:

- *Shouldn't I just be thankful for what I have?*

- *Who am I to want more when others are struggling?*

- *Am I being selfish to want a different path now?*

Let's be clear: **gratitude and desire can coexist**.

Wanting more doesn't mean you aren't grateful.

It means you're human. And growing.

🌼 You're Allowed to Change the Story Midway Through

What if this part of your life wasn't the ending, but the plot twist?

What if the story changed direction — not because you failed — but because you evolved?

You're not betraying your past.

You're **honoring who you've become**.

🧠 We're Taught to Settle (Especially With Age)

There's a cultural script that says:

"Pick a lane. Stick with it. Be thankful. Don't rock the boat."

But that script assumes your life is a **linear march toward decline**.

It's not.

You are still *becoming*.

And wanting more – joy, meaning, growth – is **a sign of life**, not greed.

📝 Try This: The "Permission Slip"

Write this on a sticky note or in big letters somewhere visible:

I am allowed to want more, even if my life looks fine from the outside.

I can hold gratitude and desire at the same time.

This doesn't mean I'm broken. It means I'm ready.

Say it out loud if you need to. Often.

Especially when guilt tries to shut you down.

▼ Bottom Line:

You don't owe the world a version of yourself that stopped growing just to keep things tidy.

You're allowed to want more.

You're allowed to go find it.

You're allowed to build the life that fits the person you are *now* – not the one you used to be.

⌛ *Chapter Seven:*

When You're Worried It's Too Late

There's this quiet fear that creeps in during midlife.

It doesn't yell. It whispers:

"You missed your shot."

"That train already left."

"You should've figured this out by now."

And because the world loves youth and speed, you start to wonder:

Is it too late for me?

Let's answer that right now.

🎓 We Were Taught to Peak Early — And Then Coast

The story many of us grew up with was:

- Choose early

- Climb fast

- Then... plateau

And if you didn't get it "right" by 30 or 40, you were behind.

But what if that story was never built for real people?

What if it was just a leftover idea from a different era — one where most people didn't even live past retirement age?

That story is broken. You aren't.

What Actually Peaks in Midlife?

Let's look at some real science for a second:

- Emotional regulation improves with age

- Vocabulary, writing, and decision-making peak later than logic and speed

- Empathy and complex reasoning *increase* in middle age

- Creativity often increases after 40, especially when you're no longer bound by early-career pressure to prove yourself. With less to prove and more to say, your best ideas may still be ahead.

- Studies show people in their 40s–60s are often *more* entrepreneurial, not less

You're not falling behind.

You're **collecting the tools** to finally do something *on your own terms.*

▣ You're Not Starting Over – You're Starting From Experience

You're not a beginner. You're a **career translator** now.

You've seen how teams fall apart and how they hold together.

You know what your red flags are – and how to avoid them.

You've worked with difficult people. Managed stress. Pushed through fatigue.

And that wisdom?

That's your new advantage.

You're not "too late."

You're just **seasoned**.

📝 Try This:
Your "Experience Equity" List

Make a list with two columns:

Everything you've done has value.

It just needs **reframing**, not rewriting.

▼ **Bottom Line:**

You are not behind.

You are not expired.

You are exactly where you need to be – to build what's next with *clarity*, *courage*, and *credibility*.

Time isn't your enemy. It's your edge.

Chapter Eight:

The Skills Journal
What You're Good At
(Even If You Don't See It Yet)

By now, you've probably had a few moments of "Oh crap, maybe I actually can do this."

That's good.

Now we need to **start proving it to yourself**.

We're going to build something I call a **Skills Journal** – your personal stockpile of:

- What you're good at

- What you've learned to survive

- What you've done so often,
  it doesn't even feel like a skill anymore

Because you've got more than you think.

Let's get it on paper.

🔍 Why This Matters

Most people trying to shift careers make one of these mistakes:

- They only look at **job titles** instead of actual **skills**

- They focus on what they *don't* know instead of what they *do*

- They think if it wasn't "official" or paid, it doesn't count

No more of that.

🧠 You've Been Learning This Whole Time

Did you:

- Mediate fights between coworkers?

- Train the new person while doing your own job?

- Lead meetings, solve emergencies, calm down angry clients, juggle deadlines?

Those aren't chores.

They're **marketable skills**.

📘 Try This: Build Your Skills Journal

Open a blank page or doc and start free-writing under these four headers:

1. **Things I'm Asked to Do Often**
   (*This shows what others trust you with.*)

2. **Things I Do Without Thinking**
   (*These are your automatic, high-frequency skills.*)

3. **Hard Things I've Handled**
   (*This reveals resilience, leadership, and creativity.*)

4. **Stuff I've Taught Others**
   (*If you've ever trained, coached, or explained something – write it down.*)

This doesn't have to be pretty.

It just has to be **real**.

💡 Bonus Tip:
Ask People Who Know You

If you're stuck, text a few people you trust and ask:

"Hey, what's something you think I'm really good at that I might not notice in myself?"

You'll be amazed at what comes back.

(And yeah, it might make you cry in a good way.)

▼ Bottom Line:

You are more skilled than your résumé shows.

More capable than your current job requires.

And more ready than you realize.

The Skills Journal is your proof.

Chapter Nine:

The 3-Factor Fit
What You Love, What You're Good At, and What Pays the Bills

There's a myth that says you have to either:

- Follow your passion and be broke
- Or settle for stability and be bored

That's garbage.

You don't have to choose between meaning and money.

You need a **fit that works for your actual life** – your family, your bills, your energy, your goals.

Enter: the **3-Factor Fit**.

⇄ The Venn Diagram of Real-Life Career Change

There are three things that need to overlap:

- **What You're Good At**
- **What You Like Doing**
- **What Pays Enough to Be Sustainable**

When those three intersect, that's your **sweet spot**.

Your aim isn't perfection – it's *alignment*.

You don't need your job to be your entire identity.

You just need it to feel like **a decent match for the season you're in**.

⚘ Step One:
List Your Strengths

(You already started this in your Skills Journal. Now build on it.)

• What do people ask you for help with?

• What have you done for years that others find hard?

• What have you trained, taught, or led?

♥ Step Two: List What You Actually Enjoy

Some of this might feel "unrealistic." That's okay for now.

- What work tasks do you *look forward* to?

- What types of challenges feel energizing (not draining)?

- If money weren't a factor, what would you love to spend your time doing?

You don't have to turn your hobby into your job — but you might find a **theme** that guides your next move.

💰 Step Three:
List Real-World Jobs That Pay

Do a little research:

- What industries pay well in your area (or remote)?

- Which job titles keep popping up when you look at postings with your skills?

- What jobs are looking for what *you* already know how to do?

This step helps ground your dream in the **actual market**.

🎯 Try This:
Build Your 3-Factor Venn

Draw three circles that overlap a little in the center.

Label them:

- **Skills**
- **Joy**
- **Money**

Then start filling them in. The overlaps will tell you a LOT.

If something shows up in all three?
You've got a winner.

If not, don't panic – this is data, not judgment.
You're just **mapping possibilities**.

Bonus Prompt: Test a Few Combos

Once you've filled in your three circles, try this:

Pick one item from each circle (Skills, Joy, and Money) and write a quick sentence imagining a career or role that connects the three.

Example:

- **Skill:** Explaining complex stuff clearly
- **Joy:** Helping people feel confident
- **Money:** Corporate training jobs pay well

→ "Maybe I'd enjoy being a learning & development trainer for a company."

Do this 3–5 times. You don't have to commit – you're just testing what combinations spark ideas.

🛠 Real Talk: You Might Not Hit All Three Right Away

That's normal.

Sometimes you start with a job that fits two out of three and gives you **space to build the third**.

Maybe you get a stable job that pays the bills *and* lets you work on your passion on the side.

Or maybe you take a short-term hit on income to build a bridge to something better.

There's no shame in being strategic.

▼ Bottom Line:

A good career shift isn't about chasing a fantasy.

It's about **connecting your strengths, your joy, and your needs** – in a way that works *for your real life*.

The 3-Factor Fit is your compass.

Chapter Ten:

Branding the New You
How to Talk About Who You Are Now

You've changed.

But the world still thinks of you as who you *used* to be.

That's not their fault – they're just working with old info.

Your job now is to **reframe your identity** in a way that makes sense to:

- Employers
- Clients
- Friends
- Yourself

This isn't fluff. It's **positioning**. And you get to shape it.

Why Personal Branding Feels Weird

You're not a product. You're a person.

So it's totally normal to cringe at the idea of "branding yourself."

But here's the truth:

If you don't shape your narrative, someone else will.

Branding doesn't mean faking it.

It means **choosing your focus** – and showing how your skills, values, and goals now connect in a way that matters.

🔄 You're Not Starting Over – You're Repositioning

Think of it like this:

• You're not leaving 20 years of experience behind.

• You're **translating it** into a new context.

If you've worked in education, you're not "just a teacher."

You're a **training and communication expert**.

If you've worked in healthcare, you're not "just a nurse."

You're a **crisis manager, care coordinator, and data specialist**.

You're not discarding your past – you're **leveraging it**.

📝 Try This: Write Your New Bio

Craft a short paragraph that answers:

- Who are you?

- What do you care about?

- What are you great at?

- What are you aiming for?

Here's a template to start with:

"After 20 years in [your field], I've developed deep skills in [your strongest skills]. I'm now bringing that experience into [new field or role], where I focus on [your new direction or mission]. I'm passionate about [what lights you up], and I thrive in roles that let me [key action or contribution]."

Use this for:

- LinkedIn

- Cover letters

- Networking

- Interview intros

- Even your own **mental reframe**

The more you say it, the more it sticks.

Bonus:
Update Your Résumé Headline

Don't just list your past jobs – start with a **summary** at the top that reflects the *current you*.

Example:

> ☑ "Strategic Communicator with 15+ years in education, now specializing in workplace training and team leadership."

It gives the reader a **lens** to view your past through.

And it helps you own your story with confidence.

🧠 Mini Exercise:
The One-Liner Identity Reframe

Try writing a single sentence that repositions your past in light of your future.

Format:

"I used to be a [past role], now I use those skills to [new direction]."

Examples:

- "I used to be a project manager – now I help nonprofits organize better systems."

- "I was a stay-at-home parent – now I coach others through complex life transitions."

- "I worked in customer service – now I teach businesses how to build loyalty from the inside out."

This isn't your full story. It's a confidence anchor.

Stick it on your mirror, your LinkedIn, or just keep it in your back pocket.

You get to own the story – and decide how it's told.

▼ Bottom Line:

You don't have to be who you were.

You don't even have to be who others expect.

You just have to be **clear and consistent** about who you are now – and where you're going next.

Branding the new you isn't bragging.

It's direction.

Chapter Eleven:

The Money Part
Planning a Shift Without Burning Down Your Life

Let's not pretend this is easy.

You've got:

- Bills
- A mortgage or rent
- Maybe kids
- Maybe debt
- And a pile of things you're trying to hold together

So when someone says, "Just quit your job and chase your dream," it's okay to want to throw a coffee mug at them.

The truth?

You can make a career shift **without destroying your stability** – but it takes planning.

Let's talk about that.

Step One: Know Your Baseline

Before you shift anything, figure out:

- **What's your bare-minimum survival number?**
  (This isn't your dream lifestyle – it's what keeps the lights on.)

- **What expenses are fixed vs flexible?**
  (You don't have to overhaul your whole life, but some adjustments may help.)

- **How long can you coast if needed?**
  (Savings, severance, support – get honest.)

Knowing this gives you power.

It removes the panic from the plan.

📉 Step Two: Minimize Risk Before You Leap

You don't have to go all in at once.

You can:

- **Build your next career in parallel** (nights, weekends, flex hours)
- **Try a side hustle or freelance project** to test the waters
- **Take a transitional role** that pays the bills while giving you room to grow
- **Use time off strategically** to skill-build or certify

This is *still a bold move* – but it's a smart one.

Step Three:
Get Curious About Compensation

Money doesn't always come from one place.

- Can you **combine income sources**?
  (e.g. part-time job + consulting + short-term gigs)

- Can you **negotiate differently** in your new industry?
  (Some fields have way better benefits or flexibility than you're used to.)

- Can you **pause** on major spending while you ramp up?

This isn't about deprivation – it's about **design**.

🧠 Try This:
Build a Career Shift Budget

Open a fresh doc or spreadsheet and sketch out:

1. **Current expenses**

2. **Income from current job**

3. **Savings / runway**

4. **New income ideas**

5. **What you'd need to make for a new job to work**

Then start playing with scenarios:

- "What if I work 30 hours instead of 40 for six months?"

- "What if I get a $2,000 contract before I leave my job?"

- "What if I don't *have* to replace my whole salary right away?"

This kind of thinking is what **turns dreams into doable steps**.

📌 Bonus Prompt: "What Would Make This Easier?"

Grab a fresh page and brainstorm answers to:

- What would make this transition feel *less* scary?

- What resources (time, people, info, money) would help?

- Where could I build a buffer – financial or emotional?

- What support could I ask for, even temporarily?

You're not just listing obstacles – you're identifying tools.

This helps shift your mindset from *"I can't"* to *"Maybe I can – with a little help."*

● Real Talk:
You Can Be
Brave and Responsible

You don't have to go broke to make a change.

You don't have to martyr yourself for stability either.

You can do both:

- Keep your life intact
- And build the next version of it

There's no shame in moving carefully.

Only in staying stuck because you were too scared to look.

▼ Bottom Line:

You're not reckless for wanting something new.

You're not irresponsible for planning it with care.

The money part matters.

And **you can handle it.**

Chapter Twelve:

Career Experimentation
Try Things On Before You Commit

There's a moment in every midlife shift where you think:

"What if I pick the wrong thing and waste more time?"

Totally fair.

But here's the trick: you don't have to pick **yet**.

This phase isn't about locking yourself into a new career.

It's about **gathering data**.

The goal isn't perfection — it's *traction*.

✹ You Learn by Doing, Not Just Thinking

You can take every quiz, read every book, and still feel unsure.

But once you *try* something – even a little – it gets real fast.

You find out:

- What you like
- What you hate
- What you're good at
- What you want *more* of

That's **career clarity** – and it doesn't come from a spreadsheet.

It comes from motion.

Try This: Run a Micro-Experiment

Think of it like test-driving a car.

You don't buy without driving. Same here.

Pick **one** small action to test a path:

- Shadow someone for a day
- Volunteer or consult for a local org
- Offer a skill on Fiverr or LinkedIn
- Teach a class or workshop
- Interview someone in the field
- Build a sample project or prototype
- Audit a course or join a short-term cohort

Make it:

- **Low risk**
- **Short timeframe**
- **Informative**

Then do a quick reflection:

- What worked?
- What felt off?
- What surprised you?

This is career research – but *fun*.

🎯 Keep What Works, Drop What Doesn't

You don't owe a new career your *entire* life to see if it's viable.

You just owe it enough time to feel the **vibe**.

If it's a no? Great. That's progress.
If it's a maybe? Keep going.

Experimentation isn't flailing – it's **strategy**.

🧠 Reminder: You're Allowed to Be New at Something

Midlife makes it feel like we should already have it all figured out.

But being new doesn't make you weak – it makes you **brave**.

So wear the beginner hat proudly.

It won't last long.

▼ Bottom Line:

You don't find your next thing by thinking alone.
You find it by **trying, noticing, and adjusting**.

Experiment like your next chapter depends on it –
Because it probably does.

Chapter Thirteen:

Flexibility vs. Rigidity
Designing a Career That Bends, Not Breaks

Let's be honest: life doesn't care about your five-year plan.

It throws:

- Health issues
- Family changes
- Layoffs
- Burnout
- Global pandemics

If your career is rigid, it can snap.

If your career is **flexible**, it can shift and keep going.

That's the difference between **chasing a job** and **designing a life**.

🧠 Rigid Careers Say:

- "This is who I am, and I can't do anything else."
- "If I lose this job, I lose everything."
- "I'm trapped, but at least it's stable."

🌱 Flexible Careers Say:

- "I have a core set of skills that can evolve."
- "If this dries up, I have options."
- "My work can grow with me."

Which one feels more like freedom?

◌ Build for Adaptability

Start asking:

- Can your skills move across industries?

- Can your schedule flex as your life changes?

- Can you pivot if something breaks?

- Can you take a pause without losing your identity?

This doesn't mean giving up ambition.

It means **future-proofing it**.

Try This: Flexibility Check-In

Take a few minutes to reflect on the career you're building.
Ask yourself:

1. Could I scale this up or down?
2. Do I have multiple ways to earn or grow in this space?
3. Does it still work if my life situation changes?

If the answer is no across the board, it's not a failure –

It's a **design prompt**.

What would need to shift to make it more flexible?

⚏ Strong ≠ Rigid

Think about the strongest materials:

- Bamboo
- Kevlar
- Steel beams in bridges

They **flex under pressure**. That's what makes them last.

Your career can be the same.

Not soft. Not unstable.

Just **built to bend instead of break**.

▼ Bottom Line:

You don't have to plan for every twist in life.

But you can build a career that's ready when they come.

Stability doesn't mean being stuck.

It means having **room to move**.

▦ Chapter Fourteen:

You're Not Starting Over
You're Starting From Experience

If you've read this far, you already know:

You're not where you were.

You've changed.

You've grown.

And now you want something more.

That doesn't make you foolish.

It makes you **honest**.

You've Been Building This All Along

Even if your past career feels unrelated, it gave you:

- Skills

- Habits

- Insight

- Stamina

- Stories

- Perspective

And **none of that is wasted.**

🛠️ Everything Counts

That job you hated?

It taught you how to manage chaos.

That boss who never listened?

They taught you what leadership shouldn't be.

That stretch where you thought you were failing?

It showed you what resilience looks like.

You're carrying all of that with you into what's next.

That's not starting over.

That's starting **from power**.

🧠 Try This:
Your Experience Inventory

Make a list of:

- 5 things you've done that made you proud

- 5 skills you've developed (even outside of work)

- 5 situations you've handled that others might have crumbled under

- 5 compliments or thank-yous you've received that stuck with you

Then sit with this one question:

"If someone else had my experience, would I tell them they're starting from zero?"

Of course not.

So don't say it to yourself.

💬 What You Tell Yourself Matters

You can frame this as:

"I'm too old to change."

Or:

"I've lived enough to know what matters now."

You can say:

"I wasted too much time."

Or:

"I finally trust myself to build something that fits."

The story you choose becomes the road you walk.
Pick one that **builds you**, not breaks you.

What Comes Next

There's no quiz at the end.

No perfect plan.

Just your life – waiting to meet you where you are now.

So go back to your notes.

Revisit the exercises.

Talk to someone.

Try something.

Start messy.

Start small.

Start now.

✳ Final Thought:

You're not behind.

You're not broken.

You're not starting over.

You're finally starting **from experience** –

And that's the strongest place you could begin.

🏁 Conclusion:

You're Already in Motion

If you made it to the end of this book, that means something important:

You didn't talk yourself out of it.

You didn't let fear win.

You didn't let doubt shut you down.

You showed up – for yourself.

That matters.

Whether you're still just thinking about a change or already in the thick of it, you've taken steps most people never do. You've questioned, reflected, and started to design something new. That's progress. That's momentum. That's courage.

No one can promise your next chapter will be perfect.

But it can be yours.

You don't need a five-year plan to move forward. You just need the next small step – and the willingness to keep stepping.

So take a breath.

Take one more look at everything you've uncovered.

And then take your next step.

You're not lost.

You're on your way.

CAN'T I JUST WANT SOMETHING *More?*

About the Author

Jennifer Larsen is an educator, author, and career coach with a deep love for helping people figure out what's next. She writes for real humans – especially those who feel stuck, uncertain, or like maybe they should've figured things out by now.

Jennifer is the founder of the Wayfinder Foundation, a nonprofit that creates and distributes practical, emotionally honest educational materials for people of all ages. Her "Can't I Just..." series is designed to meet readers where they are and help them move forward with clarity, confidence, and a little more self-trust.

She lives in Connecticut, and splits her time between writing, mentoring, launching too many projects, and daydreaming about living at Disney World.

About the Wayfinder Foundation

Wayfinder Foundation Inc. helps people of all ages explore careers, build life skills, and reconnect with who they are. Through free books, workshops, and school outreach programs, Wayfinder supports those who are navigating change – whether they're just starting out or starting over.

Learn more at wayfinderfoundationinc.org

Explore more books at cantijust.com

Other Books You Might Like

From the "Can't I Just…" Series:

- Can't I Just Stay in My Room? – A career guide for teens who don't know what they want to be yet

- Can't I Just Skip College? – Real alternatives to the traditional 4-year path

- Can't I Just Hit Reset? – A short, forgiving guide for when you've messed up

- Can't I Just Be Like Everyone Else? – Social skills for teens and young adults

- Can't I Just Help Them Fit In? – A practical guide for parents of socially struggling kids

- Can't I Just Do Something Fun? – The value of hobbies for identity, joy, and self-expression

More at cantijust.com

www.ingramcontent.com/pod-product-compliance
Lightning Source LLC
Chambersburg PA
CBHW061808120626
46550CB00005B/2194